MW01702977

MY FEARS OUT LOUD

Poems by

Maureen P. Medina

2022

JJ,
Thank you sooo much for supporting me + watching me perform. I am so grateful for you, our times together and our conversations. You are such a warm, kind + gorgeous person + you deserve all the love you give and then some. I wish you so much light, peace + joy. You deserve nothing less. ♡ Maureen ♡

Cover Art by Shane Manier, Guerilla Poets, Founder

Visit our websites:
www.ReadorGreenBooks.com
www.ShaneManier.com

FIRST EDITION
ISBN: 978-1-7378163-5-5
Produced in the United States of America

Sebastian, Noah, Dominik, Michael
Jaeson, Kennedy, Cash, Inês

Be kind.
Speak up, even if your voice shakes.

Respect boundaries.
Set them. Honor them. Especially your own.

Your feelings are valid – feel them all.
Find your peace and hold on to it.

You matter and you are always worthy.

I love you.

MY **FEARS**
OUT LOUD

Contents

HEALING, A REVOLUTION

INTRODUCTION

I once confessed to a friend that I fear everything, and they said, "It must mean that you overcome a lot."

Too often, we build others up while tearing ourselves down. We love others unconditionally - sometimes to a fault - while being unforgiving to and even abandoning the parts of ourselves that need the most love.

We are quick to hate on our perceived shortcomings that we stifle our own growth. How can we see our full potential when we are our greatest saboteurs?

I am guilty of this every waking moment and, to be honest, I am exhausted. How can I expect the most of myself while undermining my own value? It is unbearable, and this inner struggle is impossible to maintain.

I want to take accountability for and foster my own greatness, and I hope to inspire others to do the same.

I'll start here, with this book.

There's a lot that's unspoken, both dark and light, but as it is, this book is called *My Fears Out Loud.* I fear joy and peace, but I am more afraid of *not* making space for either in my life because I did not release what no longer belongs.

So here I am, sharing my fears (and hopes) out loud.

LOVE AND WAR

If someone asks you where you've been
Tell them you've been battling your demons and
you're winning.

They say all is fair in love and war, but
what if the war is loving yourself?

What if you are your own enemy, captor, *and* savior?
Is it fair then and
how do you tip the scales in your favor?

Prisoner of war,
how do you call a truce when
the army of self-doubt flanks you;
when trust, your only armor, has fallen; and
when clarity, your weapon, is lost on the battlefield?

How do you quell the rebellion of an unforgiving self?
Which wolf gets fed and which one starves?

Wave the white flag, but be merciful in your surrender.
Fear is embedded like shrapnel, but it can't have you.
Your demise is not in your defeat and
your greatest feat is fighting at all.

The war wages on but, as long as you're in it,
you're winning.

ARROGANCE

I watched a bird dip and dive
with such force, such arrogance

She flew from up high
descending with intention
A near miss as she made her way back up
just inches from the ground
I held my breath, fearing for her life

But as I watched her continue on,
dipping and diving
It occurred to me that maybe
I was the arrogant one
only cherishing life when I thought it was over,
while the bird lived in her power
for as long as she had wings.

And maybe we could learn a thing or two
about what it means to truly live.

BEGIN AGAIN

To begin again implies completion
or maybe the contrary

I begin and I begin,
though starting is the hardest part

More difficult than completion
because that requires growth, fulfillment.

And what if I fall short?
What if my best isn't good enough?

What if I remain unfinished because
the notion of completion is just too damn definitive?

On my worst days, I remain incomplete
On my best days, I begin again.

BLUSHING, WHAT A REVOLUTION

Blood rushes to my face and I am humbled
I felt cold, but now I feel hot
My neck and ears pulsating with misconceptions
They think I am timid, they think I am fragile
They think that this red can be defined
but there is no definition for my fury
I don't care if I'm misunderstood, but
I won't be underestimated
This *little girl* with the red hot face does not feel shame
I was not put in my place because

I am everywhere
I am a voice you try to suppress
I am a counter-culture
I am an anomaly and
However unfamiliar I may be to you,
I have ended the war with myself.

Here it comes again.
What a rush

I know it's coming but I can't stop it
So I count until it subsides

One Mississippi
Two Mississippi
Three...

I have learned to look forward to my peace --
Blushing, what a revolution.

DESCRIBE FEAR

My mouth is dry, hands clammy. I feel the blood warm my face, the heat radiates from my cheeks down to my neck.

Moisture on my baby hairs a dead giveaway of the first beads of sweat threatening to drip, like tears I can't cry.
Frozen, and no, I can't let it go.

My pounding heart sounds slow like waves crashing or a windy day that's so turbulent, it's like a person whistling as they stroll through the park.

Oh, I wish you were just passing through. I'd welcome a visit every now and then. You're a stranger who's made a home out of my mind -- Maybe I wouldn't mind if it wasn't all the time.

Time, what a traitor in my waking hours.
I wait in anticipation and it's as if time stands still, teasing me. When the long-awaited moment arrives, it happens so fast -- like a blur that I think I saw but know for sure that I felt.

Why do you linger? What lessons must I learn?
I can't always be a student, though you test me.
You test me and I don't know how I measure up.
I feel small, though I am big.
When I feel big, it's like I don't fit.

I won't let you speak for me.

What can possibly contain you who swallows me whole
Somehow we coexist:
One of us uninvited, the other a host
Only, I can't tell which is which.
Everything in moderation.
If only I didn't operate in extremes.

FAVORITE TIME OF THE DAY

Morning sunrise

Why does it sound like mourning when
it's the coming of a new day?
There is no grief in rebirth, in starting anew
Or maybe there is.

Unless
we're mourning the day before.
Maybe it was the last hello, the last goodbye.
Whatever happened before today is over
I guess that's why the sun sets and then rises again.

Whatever happened yesterday,
life must go on until, suddenly, we're here
in mourning.

Mourning.
Good morning.

HOME

Always a guest, but never at home
A stranger to the inner workings of how it came to be
Wish I was privy to the nick here, the nack there

Bookshelves reflect your state of mind
Art adorns all your favorite places
All the parts of the world you love
tucked away in your refuge

Everything has its place
Neat or messy - there's a method to your madness
Home, sanctuary, peace, chaos
The place, soul, sentiment, and state of being the
you that you know best

Intimacy that you can share or keep to yourself
Where you are light and dark
ugly, unfolding, unforgiving, unapologetic --
you in your entirety.

You are the most and the least,
that is your privilege
Where your secrets are safe but
never held hostage because
there are no inhibitions
no rules of being except, simply, to be at home.

I REMEMBER THE MIRACLE

Grief reintroduces itself
somehow at the door again
It manifests in tears
An ache in my belly
In the thunderous roar of anger
It manifests in waves of outbursts and calm
hopelessness
anguish
It manifests in a piercing noise or a deafening silence

Grief renders me immobile until
I find joy in the smallest movements
Until silence feels warm, and
Noise becomes laughter, perhaps my own

Until the outbursts become revelations,
Anguish becomes peace and
Anger is replaced with compassion, understanding
until the ache in my belly becomes butterflies

Grief

Though ever-present, is never alone
for there is always joy to be found

Grief is a reminder, and
I remember the miracle.

I SEE YOU

Inspired by "Let Me Come to You Naked" by Pat Parker

Let me come to you naked, fearful
My heart pounding out of my chest
So much so
That I seem transparent

Let me be vulnerable
as I stagger toward healing
How I wish I was strong enough to accept my bravery
Apologetic to myself, yet so
Unforgiving, unrelenting

I deserve better from myself
That'll show you
I mean me -- I mean us
How I should be treated

Let me come to you naked, belly up
Let me introduce my parts
All the pieces that clumsily try to fit together

Let me assume the faces that I have created
Not out of survival, but out of craving

Oh, how I long to be me entirely
How I long to know who that would be
What I would look like if I was bold enough
to peer at the mirror held up for me to see

I am more than meets the eye and as I dare to look up at myself, I say out loud: **I SEE YOU. I SEE YOU.**

JAWBREAKER

Don't make decisions when you're mad.
Just breathe through it like you're in a Lamaze class.

They teach expectant mothers how to breathe when they're
about to give birth, but

Do they brace us for the mistakes we've borne?
Do they teach us how to breathe through the consequences
of our actions?

How do we prepare for the sins we rarely confess, but always
repeat?
Repeat offenders, don't we learn our lesson?
Don't we learn through repetition?
Don't we need our bad habits to understand why we should
break them?
Better to ask forgiveness than permission, yet

We permit ourselves to behave in ways that need pardoning.
Pardon me, pardon my French,
does any of this make any fucking sense?

A penny for your thoughts, a quarter for that jawbreaker we
never finish. / We suck the color out just like that 9-5 drains
the life out of us.

Let's break the cycle, not our jaws.
Open wide, expand your horizons.
Make better choices.
Just don't make decisions when you're mad.

LOVE IS TIMELESS

Inspired by June Millicent Jordan's quote:

"How many minutes
How many hours before we agree that loving ourselves does not require our hatred of someone else?"

We see ourselves in others
We revolt when we feel shame

We are triggered by the cracks in the mirror
We are sated by the reflections we are proud of

I am you, and you are me
My ripples are yours, and yours are mine

Only when I love myself, will I love you
Only when I love you, will I love myself

Time, then, is not a question, but an answer
And love is timeless when we do it right.

PANIC ATTACK

Panic **ATTACK** Panic **ATTACK**

P A N I C

Fuel to my fire
though I need a new muse

Inspiration only strikes under pressure
Making me feel extraordinary in the chaos
Rendering me incapable of being ordinary when
I'm at peace

Can't be bothered with the minutiae
Conflate it as mundane
but my brain is
Overwhelmed, Overstimulated

Over and over
Over and over
I've learned to wait

This, too, shall pass

No more
Panic attack
Panic attack

STORM

A storm is **brewing**
I have yet to feel the calm.

My face throbs until it explodes into red
Knots in my stomach
Tingling in my limbs
I feel a surge of heat in my body

Red flames, blue flames

Fear is no longer a threat, but a certainty
It grips and contorts within me

The more I resist
The deeper I sink, but

To my surprise,
As we become acquainted

I feel the calm
Before the storm

STRAGGLERS

We squander our energy on broken souls.
Like broken glass
we underestimate the damage they do until we realize
it's the tiny pieces that cut us.
We dismiss them because they're harmless
until a prick reminds us to be thorough next time

Clean up and assess what to keep.
Don't be wasteful with your love.

Though there's no shortage,
If it spills out, the scavengers will
emerge from the sewers and come for it

They'll swarm you for every last morsel like it's theirs for the taking
They don't realize that all they do is take
They invade your sanctuary and violate your refuge
They overstay their welcome and find holes to ensure a safe return
Only, you're in danger of an infestation

Stop cleaning up a mess you didn't make
Stop validating the idea that you'll let anyone in
Stop condoning bad behavior
That's just a breeding ground for repeat offenders

Don't let them steal your warmth because
they can't find shelter
If they choose straws instead of bricks,
they should brace for the cold

Shortcuts don't make for strong foundations
A castle is built by the brave, the moat for the cowards.
You are the King, Queen, and fortress.
Let the stragglers see themselves out.

WHAT TO EXPECT WHEN YOU'RE HEALING

1. **UPHEAVAL**

You are not the same person, but you are more you than ever. Face yourself. This introduction was ordained.

2. **GRIEF**

You have lost as much as you have found.
Mourning and celebration can happen together.

3. **WAVES**

An ebb and flow of
        Truth and uncertainty
                Rage and laughter
        Safety and uproar
Noise and silence
        Overwhelm and clarity
                Dancing and crashing
        Ride the waves. Swim in them.
Revel in the cleansing.

4. **TEARS**

Ugly cry. Cry ugly. Cry beautifully. Cry joyfully. Cry.
Let all of you erupt and cascade
Let it all out and let it all in
Feel everything. This is your truth.

5. **FREEDOM**

A moment of silence to acknowledge your freedom.
What does it feel like?
What part(s) of your body just spoke to you?
Was the declaration loud or subdued? Listen.
Surrender. Rinse. Repeat.

MY PARENTS ARE HUMAN

THEY MAKE ME HUMAN

We hold parents responsible for who we are and the pain they've inflicted on us – all valid expectations. Parents are responsible for everything, the good *and* the bad. But they don't do it alone. It takes generations to make and break a child, and it is crucial to have a support system, the means to heal *and* the understanding that *we need to heal.*

We can hold our parents accountable while acknowledging the human in them, as we learn to see the human in ourselves. The following pieces are not meant to undermine the value or love that my parents have for me and my siblings (who have also been like parents to me). I hope to convey how their love - how the human in them - has shaped *my* love, and the human in *me.*

I don't intend to blame or vilify anyone with my truth. I understand that it may be hurtful, maybe even like I'm only emphasizing the pain. The hurt exists regardless of where it lives but, in expressing myself, I am no longer letting it live in me. I have finally found and created *my* safe space.
I'm holding on tight to the good, the joy, and the peace to replenish the parts of myself that need it most.

It may seem as though the bad outweighs the good, but the fact that I'm able to process, feel and identify my experience is a testament to all the good that I remember, am holding on to, and allowing myself to look forward to.

TALES

"You're a cautionary tale"
That's what I told him \ That's what I thought of her

All tales are cautionary: Fairy tales, tall tales
of who our parents are

Unforgiving because we expect better from them for
demanding better from us
Not knowing that omission and embellishment are big little
lies

There are no heroes or villains when we have the truth
but when that's stolen in our youth and we look to you,

Who can we turn to when the twisting of plots is like
Russian roulette, never know what to expect?

Doomed to repeat history, our traumas a mystery
because learned behavior can't lead to changed behavior

The only savior is taking us through the dark

I am little red riding hood
I can make it through the woods if only you told me I could
I'm Hansel and Gretel, not deceived by bad people,
I am Rapunzel and the tower's my temple, and
if you led by example then there would be
no monsters or witches, no tricks and no spells

Please stop telling tales and just tell me the truth or
the villain in the story will always be you

Please --- Just start with the truth.

I WANT ME

You want me to comply, as you did.
You want me strong, but contained.
You want me honest, but forgiving.
You want me to emulate your survival,
though you are part of my struggle.

You want me without learning me,
which helped me to discover that

I want me.

ANCHOR

Hi, mom. I'm hurting today.
And I don't think it'd hurt if it wasn't for you.

Your values are far and foreign
yet I've inherited them the way I've inherited
your temper, your smile, your strength, your resistance.

All the parts of me that I love,
all the parts that I dare to be proud of are from you.

How do I reconcile with the lessons that still torment me?
How do I make peace with who I am when you are raging
inside me, and the wars you had to survive have become part
of my story?
How can I **s e p a r a t e** us while remaining **intact**?

You are everything I've looked up to, but the more I learn
the more I understand why
you should never meet your hero

I've known you from the moment I existed, but
we've only just met.

I love you but I resent you, and I resent that I need you
I don't know how to be without you and I resent that
I wonder if that was your intention, but I still love you
I wonder if you have any idea how much you've hurt me

And how could you?

You don't know me even though I am you.

I am a reincarnation, a reiteration, a saving grace, a result of you, not proof that you left unscathed, but that you remained **WHOLE**.

The beauty is in our survival
and the tragedy lies in the trauma from generations past.
How do we end the cycle when we can't talk about it,
When you don't hear me, but your voice pervades my
thoughts and decisions?

I am haunted by the ghosts of future oppressors
that you warned me about but, when I listen carefully,
I learn that they're the ghosts of your past.

Either way, I want out. I want a new start.
If you're going to provide armor, I will let you

I need to sift through the rubble of your hurt,
your greatest fears, and find out what fits.

I can only fight with you as my armor, not my anchor.
So if you want to protect me, please *r e l e a s e* me.

DANCING IN THE RAIN

My mom never let me dance in the rain
She was told that anything could kill me because of my heart

As I got older, I feared the rain and many other things
One day, I closed my umbrella, put my things in a dry place,
ran out into the rain
And danced in it

The cold drops shocked my body
awakening my sense of wonder

I bathed in my liberation

Then, I ran to dry up in case it was true

But I didn't die
Instead, I lived.

Then it occurred to me
What else was my mother told?
What else was *I* told
that simply, was not true?

I danced in the rain
There, I found the questions.

DRESS

"I never thought you'd be so simple."
Words from my mother as we sat down to lunch.

"What's that supposed to mean?"
I chewed on my food as she chewed me out.

"Look at you. You let yourself go.
You don't wear makeup or dresses anymore.
You used to take care of yourself.
You don't care what people think. You look lousy"

"That's what you call simple?"

Don't you mean lighter, free? The me that you held with such high esteem wasn't even me
I don't want your idea of beauty stained on my face
I don't want to be your depiction of a woman,
She's the one who is blamed when a man accepts his own depiction of a man
A construct society upholds too tightly like that dress we shouldn't have worn
If we don't dress like that, then *we* look worn
And we can't risk looking frumpy

Oh, baby. Why so grumpy? You should smile more. Bite your tongue. Watch your mouth. Be polite. Be a lady.

Well, I am a fuckin' lady and then some.

I am all-encompassing.
There is no woman more woman than me just because

she wears the mask that doesn't fit her or the chains that
weigh her down.
You want me adorned with jewelry instead of good sense
Diamonds, they are bloody
They're made under pressure
No wonder they're a woman's best friend
Not valued until the pressures of who they are
grip and contort them until they cannot be recognized

Deemed unworthy until they have the
individuality snuffed out of them
They shine and sparkle -- an inaccurate portrayal of their
lackluster to be simply, just like everyone else

Put on the market, up for sale. A ploy to keep women as
property. A dowry, modern-day slavery.

Well, don't try to own me 'cause I'm not yours to keep.
And I won't be kept, mom.

Bras and stilettos, your idea of sexy. I'm complex, see
Wracking my brain for solutions beats a nice rack,
I'd rather stand tall in the battle for justice than invite
unwelcome attention, and if that's your only intention
Yes, mom. I am simple.

There's no room for expression in that frilly dress
My makeup would smear when I'm out in the trenches.

Yes, mom. I am simple. Of that I am proud.
I am loud and boisterous with my knotted hair and sweats

Strength & acceptance come in all sizes.
And that new dress you just bought me, it doesn't fit.

WHOLESOME

Mom always said to find someone wholesome.
She was whole and then some, but just in case it wasn't enough.

"Find someone with a good family, a solid foundation."

We never realized that the ground we stood on was shaky.
We just thought we danced to our own rhythm whenever the earth moved.
We found balance in skipping through the cracks, thinking we'd found our footing.

When all was still, our heads would spin.
Borne on survival mode, we didn't recognize the peace.
Was this the calm before the storm?
What to do if skies were clear and we found ourselves in sunshine?

A helping hand threw us off kilter – we were skeptical, fearful, as though we were being robbed of something.

Interlocked fingers felt like anchors, holding us down though they were there, simply, to lighten the load.

Confusing the burden lifted from our shoulders as
our armor coming off, we couldn't fathom that we were no longer in battle.

Our strength remained, substance, too, and suddenly
our movement was more graceful.

Shedding the weight left us exposed, our souls bare.
Built on pride of holding our own
we felt less than when they offered us a reprieve.
A sigh of relief, forgetting the last time we could breathe.

Fear and courage intertwined, we were whole on our own.

To let someone in meant to relinquish our freedom,
though tired from viewing everyone as strangers.

What would it take to let them in?
"*Someone wholesome,*" mom said.

"But you've been fine on your own all these years."

To which she'd reply, "*Yes, I have.*
But I would have loved to have someone to dance with."

OTHER WOMAN

When I was young, I'd spend summers with my dad
I met all of his women and they adored him
One night, I learned just how much.

I was asleep, with no concept of time.
I awoke to crying and screaming -- it was one of them.

She'd found out about his other women or maybe
she found out that she was the other woman
Not knowing that, to him, *they were all others*
and the only woman he actually wanted was my mom

The only woman with the self-respect to walk away when
my dad's eyes, hands, thoughts wandered
They could not be trusted

Still, these women, falling over each other
entrusted him with their whole being
Clamoring for this man's attention when he never had good
intentions.

So anyway, this woman pleaded with him to just admit to the
others
He was so smooth, so charming

He made her question herself even though she did the work.
Yeah, she did her homework.

Studied up on him, his phone calls
Who were you calling on the west coast when your woman is
right here with you in the east?

Who were you calling late at night when I thought I put you
to bed?

She screamed and clawed at him and he remained stoic
Refusing to admit his wrongdoing or that he was doing
anything at all

At some point,
I don't know if she knew I had woken up, but
How could I not?

She sobbed on my shoulders

I was the only one she had, the twelve-year-old daughter
of the man who forgot that she, too, was someone's daughter

As I lay there, stunned by the chaos
I remember my disgust, my utter disdain.

And you'd be surprised that it wasn't aimed
at my father.

DAD

You are half of me, yet all of me
I've inherited your charm and wit,
Your knack for helping others while overlooking yourself
You are the summers of sadness
You are the darkness I cannot overcome or speak of
You are the reason I do this work
You are the one I cannot save.

My memories as a child with you were joyful but heavy
A burden I could no longer carry, a weight I couldn't share

I looked forward to seeing you not only because I adored
you, but also because I knew that, even if only for a while,
my light would dispel your darkness

I knew I could help you carry a cross
not meant for a child to bear
Hunched over, posture ruined, I carry you and can't let go.

Every lonely person I see, every pair of sad eyes,
I feel familiar with, intimate.
I recognize you in every moment of despair.

But oh, when people speak of you
Not those embittered by this tarnished image of you they
choose to preserve,
But those who were touched by your kindness

When they speak of you, I am overwhelmed with pride.
Because this is the man I know,
The man they could not forget

This is the man I wanted to save
every summer and winter – brief windows of opportunity
not to be wasted by fun or frivolous activity.

I was a child on a mission
I sought for you and prayed for your redemption.
I sought for you in the men I dated and the men I served in my vocation.
I never found you again, except for a flicker of strength in your eyes every so often.

I didn't know, as a child or even now, what it would take to breathe life back into you.

I couldn't see the wounded child in you
No wonder you're so lonely

How could I help expel the pain that you had drowned in?
How could I go back home when my work wasn't finished?
My heart broke every time I left you

Though I missed my life, I would ache for my father.
I longed to be with you
Even in the darkness, I needed you to know that you weren't alone

It hurt more to be away from you than to be beside you
I tried with all of me to share in your pain.
Moments of joy were accompanied with guilt because
I knew you were suffering.

How could I rest when there was so much work to be done?

These were the thoughts of a child.
Rather than looking to my future, I wanted only to uncover the past - any step towards redemption.

My father, my hero.
Though the mighty fall, I swore that I'd always be there.
I would catch you, even if it meant that I fell, too.

SOFA

When I sleep on the sofa, I feel displaced
Remember when I'd visit you? Daddy's little girl.

I savored our time together
Playing cards / swimming / gambling
Finishing packs of root beer before we reached the register

I loved sleeping together
No malice in a teenager sleeping with her dad fourteen
nights out of the year
I loved our cuddles / I felt safe in your arms

But I hated when your phone would ring
I knew it was her / I knew the drill
Three in the morning
I'd pretend to be asleep, hoping you'd let me be
You'd pick me up and carry me to the sofa, whispering
"It doesn't mean anything. I'll come and get you later."

I'd hear her enter the house, and they'd shut the door.
Hours would pass by and I'd wait
Finally, she'd leave
You'd tiptoe to the sofa and carry me back to bed

The bed was warm but it wasn't safe
I knew what happened there

One time,
I put my hand under the pillow and found her thong --
Did I say one time?

I know this was your currency, but I paid, too.

TOAST

Bread and butter / the crunch, the flavor
Remind me of you

When you'd pick me up from school,
make me toast / slathered in butter and coated with sugar

When you'd braid my hair -
Mom still hasn't learned how
When you'd get dressed up
Slick your hair back and wear your
Montagut shirts, which I still can't pronounce
I just know the Filipino (mis)pronunciation
I just know you had all the colors

Toast reminds me of how you accessorize
Adorned in gold, obnoxious and endearing

Toast reminds me of
Gargoyles / Mummies Alive / swimming pools in the summer / Hercules / Xena, the Warrior Princess / naps / shoelaces / German Shepherds and Yorkies / poker / multiplication table / card games / blueberries / jasmines

Toast reminds me that I wish I had more time with you
With this least wounded version of you

Toast reminds me of
your smile / your laughter / your serenades

Please don't think I forgot.
I remember *e v e r y t h i n g.*

I ALMOST MOURNED YOU

I almost mourned you. Almost.

It was just another day, we all thought you were at work
I rolled my eyes as I rejected your call
I got your voicemail and figured I'd call you later. Or not.
"I'll just see her at home."

Then I got mom's message and I couldn't breathe.
I thought of how I'd mistreated you, taken you for granted.
I couldn't imagine life without you.
That's when I almost started mourning.

So much untapped potential / So much stagnation.
You haven't given yourself what you deserve.
This was too soon. You were supposed to move forward.
You were ready to quit, move out, do the things you wanted.
You were ready.
And those things almost happened until / you almost died.

Your life was an aneurysm waiting to happen.

An accumulation of trauma and almosts
that couldn't quite make their way out.
Your youth was so unstable / constantly changing
that you internalized movement as danger

Just as you were about to move / your body revolted
I don't know if it's because you haven't moved in years or
because you were finally going to, but
movement was the trigger and / you almost died.

You had to relearn the most basic things that forced you to
change / You had to learn to feed yourself again
how to wipe your own ass, how to walk and get dressed
You had to move, and so you did
Still, you lived / and the movement saved you.

Maybe it was a cruel joke from the universe
-- we know there's truth in every joke --
Maybe they thought it comical to force you to move --
the thing that literally put your body up in arms and
caused you to implode.

There's a reason / you almost died / but lived instead.
It's not for performative tokens of appreciation,
It's to hold you to your word.
You promised yourself that you'd change
that you'd challenge, frighten, and find yourself.

Your miracle wasn't your survival
it's in every day you get to start,
every day you get to be terrified
every day that you find new ways to heal
and give yourself the flowers you were too afraid to pick.

To know what you want, you owe yourself the exploration.
If you want love, you owe yourself the integrity of real
conversation, real connection, real let downs, real joy.

If you want to live, then do it. Live.
Change is not the enemy. It can't hurt you / it never did.

What hurt you was mom, dad and maybe even us.
What hurt you was all the hopes you had that were traded in
for bigger pictures that weren't your own.
You're in control. Change will come on your terms.

If you want safety, complacency, therein lies the danger
It means you've accepted defeat from the wrong enemy.
And to say that I almost mourned you would be a lie.
If you don't embrace yourself,
if you refuse uncertainty and hide in the shadows of your
trauma, then *I will actually mourn you.*
When I would have rather almost mourned you.

CHANGE

You tell me what excites you
You tell me what's new
Haircut / shoes / bikinis
You tell me you miss me,
ask why I don't say it back
It's not that I don't / Or maybe it is

I want to miss you, but
When I think of you, I think of why I left
I think about you all and how
I still haven't learned to separate you from them
Or me / from you

So I can't say that I miss you because
it's too early to know for certain
Where you end and where / I begin

When I think about home
I do think of you,
how I always dreamed of leaving
And then I wonder
Don't you ever want more?
Why have you never left?

As I pause to reflect and gather some compassion
for the weight that wasn't yours to bear
your inheritance --- mine
I know it's not all your fault for
resisting change when that's all you knew

THE SOUND OF YOUR FOOTSTEPS

When I was younger, I hated showering
I remember when you'd buy me scented soaps and gels
Cucumber   lavender   raspberry   melon burst
Bribery at its juiciest!

You worked so much and you missed a lot
Sometimes I'd wake up to gifts
Shirts or pants here, a jacket there
A token of, I don't know, love, surprise,
Redemption, perhaps?
You would dress me up, fix my hair and paint my face
You made the best dishes and plated them all fancy

When you were ok, we were ok -- we could breathe
I loved you so much
When you were bad, everyone suffered
When your day went wrong, we were all to blame
You were missed when you were gone, but
we dreaded your homecoming

We could tell what kind of mood you were in by
the sound of your footsteps
If they were heavier than usual, we knew you were, too.
There was no bracing ourselves for the impact

You were cruel beyond measure, still are
Yet your mind protects you from the evils we can't forget
I don't know how to forgive you because
I didn't realize how long I've been mad

I think it's as embedded in my love for you as the memories
of you that I'm struggling to hold on to

Even your tenderness came at a price
For you'd always remind us of our dues

You were entitled then and even now
You feel justified in your betrayal, deserving of our pardon
But it doesn't work like that

I don't love you because of who you are
I love you in spite of the monster I wish you weren't
How tragic that, with you, not even love is free
It comes at too high a price and has cost me my peace

I want to forgive you, but this is as far as I can go.

FOR MY FAMILY

For my mother, I'd grant you freedom that etiquette never allowed for.

For my father, I'd let you be a child instead of a crutch for your parents.

Maybe a childhood with only the expectations of being a child would have validated you and you wouldn't feel the need to find roots in all of your women

Maybe you'd find joy in your daughters instead of trying desperately for a boy to carry the same heavy load.

For my sister, I'd make you feel seen. I'd make you feel safe, heard. When he hurt you, I would have protected you. Maybe you wouldn't be so entitled to hurt others as a means of protecting yourself.

For my sister, I'd hold up a mirror to you so that you could feel all the love you give. I would nourish and replenish you, even as they deplete you.

For my sister, I'd offer courage, movement. You have found safety in hiding, even from yourself. I would grant you the will to see yourself as you are, as you could be, as you wish to be.

For my sister, I would choose you. I would love you without condition so that you'd do the same for your children.

For my brother, I would break the chains that would have you repeat history. I would reach you before it's too late and love you for you, not for the expectations of manhood, not for salvation, not for anything you may have to offer, but for all that you deserve.

CHILDHOOD

You bathed me / I was scared of the soap going in my eyes so / I'd close them / You patted bubbles on my face and made me / open my eyes / It wasn't so bad

You brought me to work / You were the only woman / at the construction site / They loved you / They respected you / But not more than I did

He made you cry / Forced you to make pancakes / Forced you to exercise / He'd make jokes about your weight / We'd all laugh / I'm sorry / I didn't stand up for you / You deserved it then / You deserve it now

We moved a lot so / I don't know how to keep house / how to keep a home / I only know that / people are homes and / when I don't feel safe, I leave / I am home

Loud as hell / always laughing / always something to say / Are we acquainted past our childhood or / have we become strangers? / I've become familiar with our estrangement but / familiarity breeds contempt / I think, soon / I'd like to get to know you.

BLOOD IS THICKER THAN WATER

Blood is thicker than water
You use it against me, grasping at straws
A last-ditch effort to bring me back into the fold

Blood of the covenant is thicker than the water of the womb

You carried me and delivered me into this world
Though I know love, though I have been nurtured
Though you know what makes me laugh --
Our familiarity ended when I lost my innocence

If only you knew what made me weep,
what keeps me up at night
what makes it impossible for me to exist in this world

If only you knew what hurt me most
the very thing that keeps me going

As my eyes opened and I chose to see
It was then I found my chosen family
Raging against violence
Begging for peace
We chose this life and, in turn, chose each other

My sisters,
We shared a womb, we share the same black hair
the same mannerisms and even the same last name

But my covenant, my people
They don't know the stories of my youth, but
they have plunged into the darkness with me

as we searched for light together

Yes, mom, you bore me
and as I fled your body and your feminine
I landed on uncharted territory
delivered right into the frontlines with warriors

They bleed with me
They mourn with me
They know me
They are me.

ISMS

ANTHROPOCENTRISM

This belief and informed behavior centers human supremacy. One of many destructive ism's.

We dehumanize our own species and, much more egregiously, dishonor the personhood of non-human animals. We forget that we, too, are animals.

Humans are disruptive and destructive to the entire ecosystem. We exploit non-human animals' existence, children, individuality, body parts, and their secretions and excretions. We exploit their parenthood, childhood, and their friendships. We exploit them to no end, to the point where we have created mechanisms that undermine nature. We play God and prioritize *our* trivial pleasures over *their* life, and *our* quality of life over *their* autonomy and freedom. We bring them into existence, and decide how they exist and how they perish.

We execute and murder them. Our cruelty is endless. It is so intrinsic to our nature, this stifling of non-human animals - that it is deeply woven into our global systems - even though it is destructive to sentient beings, the earth, and our own health. We upend our sense of morality so much so that violence has become normalized and the calls - the angry, bitter, devastated calls - for peace seem radical.

When we take a life or hold it in our hands, it's our responsibility to nurture and cultivate a safe and loving space. Instead, as per human nature, we capitalize on vulnerability. We create the notion of otherness, assign it, and then exploit it, even within our own species.

When we take time to reflect on our most basic needs, whether it's nourishment, love, affection, or freedom, they need not be named. **What we feel and yearn for are innate. We are all the same in the ways that matter.** We try to justify the abuse of any living being for how they can serve – not the greater good, but – in a way that generates profit. We try to validate the superiority of one being over another. Who gave us the authority and audacity?

If any other species were to behave like us - causing pandemics, mass extinctions, overpopulating and consuming at a rate that the earth cannot sustain - we'd consider them a virus and treat them accordingly.

Our souls are not beyond redemption, but our moral compass is off kilter and we must be redirected so that we can acknowledge our complicity. With every purchase we make, everything we are a part of - and this is for those who can afford to change - we are complicit in some form or another. There are many evils in the world. Rather than being despondent or nihilist, or insisting only on our individual happiness, we must acknowledge how our lives affect others'.

For those who are able to reflect, rebel, protest, and denounce - I challenge you to truly examine your lifestyle and privilege and ask yourself if your joy, comfort and peace cost someone theirs. Does your self-gratification cost lives?

RACISM

I'm the darkest in my family and my features are different, so I was raised on micro aggressions. **I've only recently recognized my/our (internalized) racism as a(n ongoing) result of white supremacy.**

I've always considered myself an ally to fellow people of color (POC), but I never felt connected to my Filipina roots until COVID or after the spa shootings in Atlanta, which triggered panic and anxiety whenever I left home.

I realized my privileged of having this ease - the levity of existing in peace without being in danger or fearing it. This helped me to finally (but still not fully) identify with fellow POC - how they are vilified and their misrepresentation as monsters and terrorists is informed by deep conditioning.

Individuals and communities are systemically destroyed and they dare to defy and dismantle the violence that destroys their families and spirit. Rather than acknowledging the source of their rage, the violence is so normalized that we fixate on their reaction rather than the evil to which they are reacting to.

Be an ally by disrupting violence, addressing racism (& all isms) however possible, and amplifying – not co-opting – their spaces. Recognize your complicity and learn from it.

Whether it's against yourself or others, whether it's implicit or explicit biases; once we know better, we must do better. **It is our privilege and responsibility.**

HAPPY ENDING

Happy ending.

Is that what you came for when you sought my people out
because you had a bad day?
Fetishizing my existence and eliminating me,
simply because you couldn't control yourself?
Your white supremacy could not be contained.
Shots fired!

Hatred in every bullet, yet we've died many times before
When you came to our countries uninvited
our beds unsolicited, our cultures that you appropriated and
then sold to us as a sign that you were here.

Children borne from a lack of protection.
Colonization - is that a justification or an ultimatum?
You forced us into your melting pot, watching all the colors
become one, dividing us with a gradient.
White is right, but yellow is the next best thing.

Stand back, Tiger mom.

She vilifies blackness as though it's dirty, ugly.
But black lives matter and they are beautiful.
We are beautiful.
And no, brown is not lesser than; brown is not illegal; brown
is not lazy.
We are brown, too, and we work hard.

We provide for our own and we -

"Stop!" Tiger mom won't have any of it.
"*We are not them*, she says. "*We earned our way*."

Good at math. Straight A's. Straight hair.

Typecast, though we are black, we are brown, and we are indigenous.
We are every single color, texture, and blessing.
We are not a monolith, and we are storytellers if we believe the myth of the model minority.

Hey, how do Asians name their kids?
Just drop a bunch of silverware down the stairs and listen to the sounds they make.

Ching Chong. Chink. Gook

We are the punchline, but we respond with obedience.
Loyal to the monster that mocks chinky eyes and seeks the crease in our eyelids without ever questioning how a colorful society can brim with oppression & individual suppression or how a colorblind society overlooks what it won't put a name to:

RACISM. XENOPHOBIA.

How can we call them strangers when we have all met before?
Hate crimes, all different iterations of the same sentiment that we are other, we are less than, and we are stained by color.

Distorted by your concentration camps, cheap labor, and conditioning
You pit us against each other and run away without incident.
You loathe all things *foreign* and call us essential while you try to erase us.

We adjust and adjust, our assimilation irrelevant to your contempt for all things *Made in China.*

Well, the whole world is watching, and they know what you have done.
They see who you are. They know that you --

You have thrived from our stolen freedom and
you are not a disease
you are not the exception
you are not a mental health issue
you are not a disability
you are not a broken childhood
you are not a bad day.

You are our friend, lover, spouse, neighbor, sibling, parent,
nurse, doctor, lawyer, judge and jury

And you are the problem.
You are violence perpetuated.
You are the stigma.
And you.

You: misogynist, white supremacist, colonizer, oppressor,
racist, terrorist. You ---

You were made in America.

I AM THE EXCEPTION

"I am the exception," I say
I thought that this admission,
this rejection of self made me exceptional
when it only made me complicit
Asian or American, you won't let me be both
Internalized racism, another cog in the system
White supremacy at it again.

"I am the exception." I'm not like most Asians.
I am loud and boisterous; I have a Spanish last name
I get real dark in the summer; My hair is thick and wavy
I don't have Asian friends; I'm not like most Asians

"I am the exception." I'm fluent in English.
Conversant in other languages, but I don't know my own
I'm not like most Asians

"I am the exception." I don't date Asian men.
They're too feminine, small dicks and
do they even know Kung fu?
You fetishize me the way I cancel them
I'm not like most Asians

"I am the exception." I am not submissive.
I am not invisible, but I am weighed down and battered by
generations of trauma where
self-harm was a form of survival

"I am the exception." That's what I say
because that's what I've been told
But I will not hate myself -- I will not hate at all.

I will love myself enough to unlearn and then learn that
there is more to me than being othered
there is more to us than being exceptional

There is history of violence and hate crimes, colonizers and erasure; There is history of division amongst people of color that you cultivated.

There is history of rebellion, unity, uprisings and success
There is history of warriors, healers, nurturers, survivors

Terrorists only see color, their lack of vision enhances ours
We see through the smoke and there is glory to be found
in the richness of our cultures; our victories, big and small
in our friendships, allies, and the fact that we're still here

Their hate is overwhelming but it is not enough
So the next time they dare to other me,
The next time they hide behind my "resilience"
I will say, "*I am not the exception.*
I am your greatest fear, proof that you'll never win.

Wala kang hiya. Alam mo ba kong sino ako?
Awan babain yo. Amammon no assino-ak?

I'm Filipina American.
My dad's from Manila and my mom's from Ilocos City.
I am proud of my roots and I am me in my entirety.

Pagtangtangsit ko ti naggapuak. Adda-ak idtoy nga agnanayon.
Puring puri ako sa ninuno ko. Habang buhay, nandito ako.

USE YOUR WORDS

Violent when violated
"*Use your words*," they said.

But I always talk with my hands.
That's how I make them understand

That I will never again be violated
even when you get violent.

THE RED TENT

Inspired by The Red Tent, by Anita Diamant

Dinah leans in and whispers, "*Speak up.*"

The power in her silenced voice
embodies the duality of women as
coveted creators of life *and*
those whose life does not belong to them

Virgins or whores, the narrative favors the storyteller
You defend our honor because you've made it your own

Obey your mother, protect your sister
Love them at all costs
We still haven't learned that freedom can't be bought

What to do with your
lovers and wives, and the mother of your children?

Their value changes with their cycles
More than bloodshed, it's a massacre
How they mutilate our bodies
Ravage our existence
Claim our birthright

Though you are bound to your
Phallic fallacy -- a fantasy

Our truth is absolute
And that is, we are free.

OATMEAL

"*What's for breakfast*?" "Oatmeal," I said.

The conversation that would follow was just another day, another trigger.

It would also be our end, reminding me why breakfast is the most important meal of the day.

"*What's for breakfast?*" "Oatmeal."

I feed myself a mouthful. Chew. Swallow. Repeat.

"*What are you really doing?*"
"I told you. I'm eating breakfast."

"*No, you're not. You're sucking someone's dick.*"
"No, I'm not. I'm eating oatmeal."

Accuse. Deny. Gaslight. Swallow. Repeat.

This would be the first fight on our last day together.
A wholesome breakfast saved my life.

NO MEANS NO

NO MEANS NO / Whisper it, say it, scream it out loud!

NO MEANS NO
I do not consent, I do not agree, I do not give permission
I do not know the full extent of what you are asking so
I can't possibly say yes. Access denied.

My boundaries transcend human connection so that
I may continue to have connection
My boundaries are constant, unwavering
Only I can enforce them.

NO MEANS NO / It does not discriminate, whether you are a friend, foe, or stranger

NO MEANS NO / It's not just about sex
Assault comes in many forms
like manipulation, coercion, and micro aggressions
It's invisible. It has no odor, no taste, but it is ever present.
It knows you better than you know yourself.

Assault happens when they can't or won't take no for an answer.

When they take advantage of the kindness of a stranger or, worse, a loved one.
When they disagree with a choice made against their will or take it away altogether - a choice that isn't theirs to make.
When they abuse the words "I'm sorry" as much as the person they say it to
When they fool you once, twice, robbing you of informed consent.

You think you know them.
You think you know what you're saying yes to.
That is assault -- it is cunning.

It's when our naïveté has us saying yes to a life we could never imagine, not even on our worst days.
When, to us, insanity is doing something over and over again and expecting different results but, for them, it's patient entrapment.

Assault is when they expect the best from someone while holding them responsible for the worst.
When they violate our existence, and then claim it as their own, as their right.
When they underestimate our power and they fear it.

And how many times have we heard the word **NO** when we wanted, needed a yes?
How many times have we been honored when we said **NO**?

Assault is a pattern of behavior. It is repetition.
It is controlled, contained and conniving.
It is gross disrespect of one's free will.
It is the assumption that no is not an option.

But sometimes, **NO** is the only answer I have.
It's the only answer to give, the only weapon I can wield.
And I'm learning how to use it.
Often, freely, without explanation.
NO.

WORTH

Let's talk about worth.

Am I unworthy because I don't have curves?
Am I unworthy because I've never given birth,
borne a child, our future generation?
Am I unworthy because my breasts have never swelled up
with milk, nourishing another?
Am I unworthy because my uterus is empty, vacant, for as
long as I can help it?

Say I did all those things and was all those things?
If a female produced a life with the power that is *her* --
If a female gave sustenance to a child, innocent and fragile?

What if, because she provided for them, loved them, and
raised them, they became strong and beautiful?
Would she be worthy then?
Then why do you feast on those who are worthy?

Why do you dig your teeth into someone's child and feed
them to your own?

Why do you demand the milk from their breasts when you
no longer suckle on your mother's?

What entitles you to the body, soul and essence of a being
just because you need something to spread on your toasted
bagel, a little sweet for your black coffee?

What entitles you to crispy, carcinogenic strips, accompanied
with the menstruation of another being - sunny side up?

A breakfast of champions, you call it.

Are you the champion of broken families,
mass destruction of forests,
depletion of earth's natural resources, and
unspeakable cruelty?

Please tell me, how do we assign worth?

Can we honor it by not commodifying it?
Who is worthy? Think about that

and then act accordingly.

FEAST

What a feast!
Oh, the smells.

Lechon, deep-fried pig.
Sans rival, my favorite cake.
Crispy, creamy, melts in my mouth.
Tilapia, extra crunchy with garlic fried rice
The kind where the rice sticks to the pot

Another celebration with all things familiar
Only now, I see things differently.

That deep-fried pig once screamed for their life
Forced into gestation crates or castrated at birth
Lowered into gas chambers for an unforgiving death

Cake, so rich and decadent
I have befriended cows rescued from slaughter
Did you know that they're pregnant for 9 months, like us?
Have you ever heard a mother cry out,
bellowing for her child?
I have seen a pregnant mother murdered on a truck
Her child cut out of her womb, then tossed into the trash
Is this how we treat motherhood?
Is this worth celebrating?

Fish!
I'd devour every part, sucking the flesh out of their eyes and
brains – Yes. I, too was complicit in their
asphyxiation and their organs exploding from the pressure of
being desired but not valued.

Imagine searching for food - the most basic instinct -
only to learn you've been tricked?
What a slap in the face --- No, a stab in the face --
as you gasp for oxygen, liberation.
What if your silence was perceived as lack of sentience?

What a feast! What a travesty.

LIFE, LIBERTY AND THE PURSUIT OF LIFE AND LIBERTY

America is under attack! Let us pray.

In the name of the father, the son and the Holy Spirit
Please God, protect the supremacists
MAGA terrorists, *better known as patriots*
Alt right, white is right
To hell with their colored compatriots
Camp Auschwitz, erase the indigenous
6 million wasn't enough
4 centuries and counting aren't enough
Insurrection wasn't enough
Impeachment wasn't enough

Let's ask McConnell
Blue lives matter except at the capitol
USA, KKK, parlay
What did the Fox say?
It's all on Parler

They say *all lives matter*
Except the black ones
Except the brown ones
Except the female ones
Except the trans ones
Except the queer ones
Except non-human ones

All whites matter
This isn't the America they know
Borne of justice and peace for their kind

But there is no justice, no peace
When we are murdered in our sleep
When we say we can't breathe
When our necks are crushed by knees
Gunned down wearing hoodies
Gunned down buying candy
Destroyed for existing

Systematic genocide
Stand back and stand by
Orders by 45, who's now been impeached twice

Stop the steal! Yes, stop the steal
Stop stealing the peace of a fairly won election.
Concede. We chose Biden.
Stop stealing lands and identities and calling it colonization
Stop appropriating our culture, our grief, and calling it assimilation
Stop stealing our dignity - or attempting to - because that's straight up degradation
Stop your stealing, suppressing, and sedition

Stand back and stand by
Orders by 45, wholly incapable of abiding by democracy
Incite all the proud boys and girls
Grab 'em by the motherfucking pussy
Including the first female VP
Oh, Harris. They want the sugar without the spice

You are the first in the house but not the last
Shatter the glass - there is no ceiling
Let's move forward. Please, no blasts from the past
No more mass deportation. No more mass incarceration
Let's change the system where the currency is our lives

Change the climate from ICE to FIRE
Because we've been hungry long before the strike
And if hate is all we've got
Where does that leave our melting pot?
Scorched with gunshot residue

This election can't just be another shot in the dark
Enough with the oligarchs who condemn anarchy
while inciting violence and misogyny

In a country
Divided by rhetoric that fits in a 280-character limit
There are no filters, there are no limits
Tweet-sized FASCISM.

Shhhh, shhhh. Can't we all just get along?
Left, right - Let's put aside our differences because we are all very special.

"Go home. I love you."

HARLEM

Inspired by "Harlem," by Langston Hughes

In white america, where your *dreams are deferred*
We don't care if you're black, but it's not preferred
Where they dry up **I can't breathe**
Put your hands up **I can't breathe**

Raisins in the sun, but not too much sun
Racism kills our black sons
All moms were summoned when he called for just one

They fester like sores
Protesters / Pro - testers
Test the crowd , make them go wild
Don't run or they'll shoot tear gas, blind the masses
Anti-racist, anti-fascist

Hate stinks like rotten meat
Like the 13th amendment: a claim to end slavery
But always read the fine print
Mass incarceration, black criminalization
And if you speak up, there goes the first amendment

Until they crust and sugar over like a syrupy sweet
He incites violence with nonsensical tweets
Justice for all, land of the free!
"Dominate," he said. "Crush his neck with your knee"
Inflammatory rhetoric, sanctioned brutality

And hate sags with a heavy load
A weapon of mass destruction,
Systemic oppression in tow.

Your racism is showing: Amerikkka's 'bout to implode
When windows are broken, it's all over the news
But bring on the lynching, Trump readied the noose

Arrest the cops that killed Breonna
Hunt for George Floyd
4 centuries captured in 8 minutes
Skin color: yeah, they weaponize it.

Silence is violence, so I'll say this out loud:

NO JUSTICE, NO PEACE.
NO JUSTICE, NO PEACE.
NO JUSTICE, NO PEACE.

SYNESTHESIA

Synesthesia

The beauty of seeing colors in music or music as colors
The perception of togetherness
for there is no one without the other

Why is it that, when you see color, you don't see me?

The sun beams down on us, reminds us of its power,
but you won't be humbled.
You cling to the shadows and that is darkness I won't
tolerate

Souls fade into a gradient sorted by rose-colored glasses
and they'll burn you to ashes
with their pointy hats and sticks or batons
and tell you color is wrong, well

The only time white is right is when it's a blank canvas,
a clean slate unstained by your dirty mind

WE'RE BLESSED BECAUSE WE'RE GOOD

The symbol for victory now stands for peace
But isn't peace victory?

And what is peace? Is it the absence of grief
stricken, fallen from grace
like *Lucifer*

Was he always a villain or was he vilified because
he defied God who said
"Thou shall not play god or worship false gods"

We cry out for all deities but
the only one who hears us is Hades
"*Thou shall not use god's name in vain*" even when
We call out for Him in vain
as we sink into the quicksand that is   life

Are we headed to hell or are we already there?
Are we trapped in karmic captivity?
Are we either good or bad with no in-between or
does strife reflect our duality?
Are we doomed or
Is there always room for redemption?

My mom always said,
"We're blessed because we're good."

So what does that say about everyone else?

RESISTANCE

I'm starting to think that resistance is the root of all evil.

When we resist others by regarding them as such, and then
sabotage their quality of life or right to live, there is struggle.

When we resist reality, that is, normalizing violence
Making peace a radical notion, strife persists.

When we resist someone's truth because it's not our own
When we reject their pleas to do better or,
at the very least, the right thing, we lose our decency.

And when we resist any being's right to bodily autonomy
When we resist their equity and freedom
and exploit them until they are reduced to their parts

When we resist the inherent value of life because
death has more capital, we have lost our way.

We are so far gone that

The earth is quaking
The fires are raging
The waters are flooding, swelling, inundating, and retreating
The humans are revolting
And all other life is weeping as they perish -
Extinction, a welcome end

Even then, with scorching winters and ice cold summers
We resist and resist, though resistance

Resistance is futile.

PERSIMMON TREE

I came back to find the fallen persimmon tree
And as I stood, marveling over the travesty of human greed

I did more than grieve the persimmons - juicy and abundant - that you would never bear again

I mourned the life that no longer was and wondered why most things – most beings – are only valued when they're dead.

HOLY

You're acting like an animal
You eat like an animal
You treat me like an animal
You work me like a dog
You're a fucking rat, a snake, sheep
Police are pigs

Why do we other, vilify, & degrade our fellow animals as if they are not us?
As if they are not also parents, siblings, lovers, friends?
As if they don't also love, fear, and grieve?

How can we denounce their personhood, their value, when we depend entirely on exploiting them?
They are just like us when it suits us, they are nothing like us when it doesn't

They are sentient beings.
who are kind, caring, selfish, and complicated, just like us.
They matter whether we believe it or not, and

Who are we to play God when a loving God would never hurt their children?
Who are we to play God, breeding life into existence only to snuff it out as we see fit?
Who are we to play God and decide who lives or dies, who is free and who isn't?
Who are we to play God when our maltreatment of others also hurts ourselves?

We revolt when powers are abused,
when life is taken for granted and treated as pawns.

In the same breath, we deny someone their autonomy,
we ravage the female reproductive system, we rip into childhoods as we sink our teeth into their flesh,

we displace families both human and non-human alike,
we prey on the most vulnerable to do our dirty work - crimes
we wouldn't dare to do ourselves

We cause physical and mental health disasters and then have
the audacity to stigmatize trauma, substance abuse, and
"criminal" activity

We steal land, oxygen, water,   life.
We have normalized violence to such a degree that the
notion of peace feels radical.

Love your neighbor as you love yourself.
Do not steal. Do not kill.
Treat others the way you want to be treated.

This is godly. This is holy.

If we were made in God's image, if we are doing God's work,
if unfathomable cruelty is what God asks of us,

What would the devil have us do?

PERSONAL CHOICE

I can't help myself.

You feel so good. You taste so good.
You scream and writhe in pain as I have my way with you.
But I can't help myself.

I love the way you feel, so soft.
I love how you smell when you're almost ready.
I crave you, in my mouth, on my skin.

You don't want this, but you were made for me.
You were made to serve me.

I try to be strong and have something, someone else.
But I've been conditioned to believe that I can,
should   have you at a whim.
Sometimes you make me sick, but I want you anyway.

Your mother begs me to stop, wailing in agony
A noise that can't be identified.
Your babies cry for you, beg for your release, for theirs.
I've heard this countless times before, their pleas falling on deaf ears.

This is my personal choice and you belong to me.

You belong to *me*:

Pig / Cow / Chicken / Fish / Lamb / Goat / Crab / Lobster /
Duck / Shark / Goose / Coyote / Horse / Mink / Rabbit / Bee

All of you non-humans. *You belong to me.*

Nothing but commodities, something *not* someone.
You are my slave and I am your captor.
You die for me. All for my *personal choice.*

EASTER

You watch me closely, curiously.
You're drawn to me and, as you take one step and then two towards me, you feel no fear

When the man with the apron comes, you tense up
Your eyes shift and you feel yourself backing up and away into your friends who are also trying to flee.
When there's nowhere to run, you turn back and our eyes meet again

You can discern between light and darkness, and your confusion lies in why you can't be with me
We keep a steady gaze, though my eyes are now filled with tears
You make a sound, soft and friendly, initiating a conversation I wish wasn't necessary -

"Hi, there. I don't know you, but I do. I'm scared. I'm so, so scared and I don't know why I'm here. My friends, they're all sick and they're scared, too.

These men, they... they take my friends one by one, but none have ever returned. I hear them crying and I don't know whether to help them or myself.

I don't know why they treat us this way, but I know that I want to go with you. Please, take me with you."

Just as I swipe another tear from my cheek, they all rise up in a chorus of pleas.
I look them in the eyes - acknowledging the individual in each of them - the only act of love I can offer.

I take a step forward, and so do they.
A worker comes and they retreat.
We do this dance until, finally, the worker says to me,

"Listen, I know why you're here. Pick one, I won't tell a soul."

I thought this would be the easiest part but it's the hardest. If I left them all behind, at least they'd still be together.

How do I choose which one lives?
Is it based on their personality?
Who's smarter? Who's healthier?
Or should I pick the smaller one or the weaker one?

I came here powerless, now your life rests in my hands.
Which one will be free and which one must die?

My mind is racing, my heart threatening to burst.
Beads of sweat drip down my face and then the worker says, "Hurry, my boss is coming!"

I don't realize that I'm still crying until I taste my tears.
Mindlessly, my hand shoots up as I point a finger at one.

The worker walks to the one I chose but this time is different.
Instead of fleeing, the chosen one comes closer, easy to grab.
They all come close thinking that they've been spared.
As the worker hurries over to me with a child, he tells me to leave.
Before I do, I look back at them. Watching, waiting.

"Is this it? What about the rest of us? Please help. I'm so scared and so lonely"

But I'm almost at the door and I plead with them, "I'm so sorry."

As I look down at you in my arms, you're crying, too.
I don't know if it's relief or guilt, but the impossible has happened and you're alive to feel both.

Seconds pass, and then minutes, days, weeks, and months.

You're settled in your new home, free to roam and have a life that belongs to you.
And though the others were murdered before you fell asleep in my arms, they will always be alive to me.

Their eyes, their pleas, the life in them -- they haunt me.

As I celebrate your life, which means the world to you,
I lament the reality of what you narrowly escaped.
I mourn for those I did not choose who, in my mind,
I sent to slaughter myself.

I feel a deep, guttural, maniacal rage that I cannot cry, laugh, or scream out. I feel ---

And just like that, my privilege is clear.

I am still here. I'm hurting, but I still exist and as long as I do then this story is about you in my arms who will live out a full life
and you and you and you, who I could not choose that day.
That day is over and you are all long gone. But choices must still be made.

So now I ask you, you who are able, you who have the power to choose.

I choose who lives and you choose who dies.
But how did your personal choice become mine?

TIMES SQUARE

Times Square, lights flashing
in the city that never sleeps
Pulsating with capitalism

I stand on the red steps & watch how life whizzes by
In awe of normalized violence at every turn

Dallas BBQ,

ribs are ripped from pigs who are castrated at birth
Their bodies are slammed repeatedly, the cheapest way to
destroy them -- all without anesthesia

Those Henny wings
There's not enough Hennessy in the world to numb the guilt
of a slaughterhouse worker
or the pain endured by day-old chicks deemed useless
Tossed into a macerator and ground up alive.

They take flight for the first and last time -
proof of their will to live.
The surviving victims' beaks are seared off, and that's just
the beginning of their miserable lives.
This clean, lean meat you eat? They cannibalize.

Red Lobster

How about them crustaceans?
Boiled to death and, though we mistake their silence for lack
of sentience
they feel every pang of pain longer than it takes for you to eat
their tortured bodies

Their screams can't be heard, but you'll never stop hearing
mine

Cold Stone Creamery

A serenade with every purchase
Have you ever heard a mother beg for her child when they
are stolen from her the minute they exit her
battered body?
The umbilical cord still attached to a child who suckles on
the fingers of the one assigned to execute them

Yes, humans are also victims, and there are
some sins you can't come back from

So don't ask me if I care about humans and don't say I shove
my beliefs down your throat because if you believe it's right
to slit a child's throat well then

I hope you choke on the hypocrisy, because
I call 'em as I see 'em and if that's extreme then
I'm radical.

We are all animals.
Please.

STOP EATING CHILDREN.

TRANSPARENT

If you had glass eyes,
would they make you transparent?

Would they shatter
Shatter and splinter, blisters
from trying to clear my vision
What a mission
A sight for sore eyes

I hear the cries of what happens when
the sheer force of

being human wipes out humanity.

MEET YOUR MEAT

Meet your meat
It's a meet and greet
You beat your meat as they meet their fate
End up on your plate

Meet the guidelines set by the USDA
Meet the oncologist, meet the cardiologist
who say eating meat is OK
even when their DNA mutates every time we play GOD

We swap meat at the swap meet
and that meat you can't live without
must live without meeting their young
So savory on your tongue, the dung of your meat
is why the heat rises - It's a crisis
The climate has met its match

Meet the "monsters" we name as thieves, though they are neither
We say they take our jobs when, instead, they take lives and their hands meet as they pray for
Pardon me

There's no meeting halfway, we are past the tipping point
Millions have nothing to eat, their food is fed to your meat
Land and water loss for your meat
Destruction for as far as the land meets the sea
Trees gone for your meat and soon
you'll be struggling to breathe like the meat that you eat
They stick and they meet your organ
Failure, so much erasure and we blame it on culture

We ravage nature and it's not natural
When we harm one, we harm all
But you never meet your meat
until they're packaged nice and neat

From their ass to their feet, your afternoon treat

You say it's cheap, more than leafy greens
Soon you'll meet your maker
but first, a pacemaker for your ticker, your heart
Meet the flicker, the spark burning down the amazon
All hands on deck as you slit the neck of the one
You'll never meet. Bleed them out
That's what happens for meat – slabs on the grill

Fires raging for the kill, ignited by your appetite for meat
Their life ends when your craving begins

If eating meat is personal, shouldn't we ask the individual
who we never meet until they become meat?

I'll meet you at the crossroads to reflect on the
true cost of meat instead of asking,
"You care about pigs, but what about Pete?"

What else can I say?
DAMN, YOU LOVE MEAT!!!

NO COMEMOS NIÑOS

No comemos niños.
No comemos niños.

Ay, lo siento ¿Está confundido?
Sí, sí. Lo puedo repetir.

Cuando me preguntas si yo como carne, te contesté:
"No, no comemos niños."

Sí, en serio. Te dije que no comemos niños
No debemos comer nadie.
Me miras como tengo una diferencia
Pero es necesario a decir que **no comemos niños.**

Quizás no son tus hijos o hijas,
pero los bebés tienen padres y familia.

Los bebés no ya tienen algunas meses antes de los degollan.
Robamos sus derecha a libertad y tambien su calidad de vida.
Robamos sus familias, amistades, y amor.

LADRONES.

Robamos todo y la única cosa que necesitamos de los
animales non-humanos es su perdón
Cuando la violencia no es normal pero está normalizada,
Tengo que preguntarte, a todos ustedes

Vete a casa, besa y abraza a tus hijos y entiende que
tu tienes el poder de decidir si alguien vive o muere
pero cada día, cada comida, te quitas una vida.

Compañeros, te lo ruego. ¿No tiene vergüenza?

LOUD

The loudest things have a different kind of permanence

Fireworks that turn summer nights and holidays into /
trauma / Diamonds that illuminate a woman's hand but cost
a child theirs

Malls and resorts, fun amusement parks / What a life / What
leisure / How many displaced beings made homeless?

Humans and non-humans / Refugees / forced to disperse
while the invaders treat them as visitors / intruders

On second thought, maybe it's not the loudest things, but
manmade things that have a different kind of permanence
because

The sun is loud and it gives life
Storms thunder and boom, and when it rains, it pours
When the bees buzz, it means we still have a chance,
however grim
Like roots breaking in that ultimately bear fruit
and flowers that bloom, without needing much
Ants marching in line,
underwhelming but invaluable to our ecosystem

Oh, how we overlook the calls of nature

Like the boy who cried wolf
no one believes the truth tellers and the truth seekers:
life savers in their own right
We hear but we don't listen
reason drowned out by false gods

They tell us in big, shiny packages that
we need this and we want that

Oh, how their cries are as deafening as the ones that are
silenced
Warnings wailing in the wind, in the hurricanes, the
earthquakes, tornadoes and droughts
Plagues and pandemics,
when will we learn?

The loudest things have a different kind of permanence.
Humans, a most potent virus
The more we multiply, the more we destroy.
We are loud, boisterous and intrusive and
our fellow beings weep as we suck the life out of them

LOUD, LOUDER, LOUDEST as the war wages on
between humans and humanity

King Midas turned everything into gold but / with just one touch / we make everything old and extinct / the only race we're winning.

Time, our only captor, cannot be bought.
Time reminds us that we are mortal and
oh, is it coming for us.
Time will save us all.

HURT

It hits me in the stillness
grips me with no sign of letting go

I don't claw my way out of darkness because
I'm so used to running to it

Sometimes silence is my self-preservation
because I have no more words to express my grief

If you cannot face the monstrosities of which you are
complicit then there is no picture I can paint, no way to
articulate the sorrow of which you are the source

Though they are not voiceless, I save my words for them
We don't speak the same language, yet I have heard those
cries before from one person to another

Their pleas for mercy – the desire to live – is universal
It does not discriminate, though you do

In the depths of despair, the will to live still lingers,
in the same way their broken bodies cling to yours

Karmic captivity, for in destroying them
you destroy yourself and the world over

Their cries are muffled by your refusal to change,
drowned out by the machines of destruction,
the sharpening of knives and the sizzling on the pan.

You hear but you don't listen

That's why silence is my weapon and my savior
I wield it wisely and use it to take cover

Silence is violence but only when we're silenced

and if I break mine, that means you broke them,
which leaves me broken

Silence is all I have when I'm screaming inside

Silence is deafening but only when the trucks have been
unloaded and the crates emptied

Only when the last one has perished,
their resilience no match for your indifference,
as you took what wasn't yours in
your blood-stained hands

I speak up when I can but
my silence conveys multitudes

Is silence the calm before the storm, or the aftermath?

THINGS THAT MAKE THE WORLD STOP

The things that make the world stop are the very things that keep it going:

LOVE / HATE
COWARDICE/ COURAGE
LOSS / REDEMPTION
LIGHT / DARK

CELEBRATION / TRAGEDY
CONFUSION / CLARITY
BITTERNESS / SALVATION
HOPE / FEAR

THE INDIVIDUAL / THE COLLECTIVE

The things that make the world go round will bring us to our knees

It's too late to ask questions we don't want the answers to
Things that make the world stop.

THESE HANDS

These hands of mine
What are they good for?

Gentle enough to braid my child's hair
Tender enough to caress my partner
Strong enough to provide for my family
But these treacherous hands betray my soul.

These hands are providers.
My loved ones rely on them, not knowing what they have done, what they do. Every single day.

They don't know how these mangled hands
take lives just to sustain ours.
They don't know that these hands, though washed so many times, will never be clean.
They will never be absolved,
not even addiction can make me forget.

These broken hands of mine make for a broken home.
An unforgiving system that hates who I am, but preys on the power of my hands

What else can I do? Given neither flowers nor skill

These guilty hands are paid to destroy, and *I* am a casualty,
my family is a casualty.

The ugliness to which my hands were complicit has cost me,
us, peace.

These hands pray for atonement for what they've done, but
not even prayer can bring the dead back to life

These hands. Assassins.

These hands hold children, fragile and full of promise,
in one hand; and darkness in the other.
The only promise is hurt for all of us.

Some fight until the end, determined, *hopeful.*
Some are so terrified, they don't move.
They don't make a sound.
They cower so low, trying to be invisible.
Their only hope is that we don't find them
They know that *these hands* made their friends disappear.

It's up to these hands of mine to bring them back to reality.

And, while they scream out in terror, resistance
everything I can't afford to express --

These hands, they kill.

A tribute to slaughterhouse workers.

SUN-KISSED

The sun kisses my face
I instinctively tilt my head back and close my eyes.
A split second, but everything stops and I feel free.
Everything else is suspended, irrelevant, as
I bathe in the light, healing.

Every time the sun kisses my face, I think about yours.
Have you ever felt the sun? Have you ever felt peace?

Suddenly, grief. Overwhelm.

Where do I begin?

Were you scared? Did you fight?
Did you have a friend to cling to?
Were they ripped from you, or you them?

As I think about my dreams, the life I envision for myself and my partner, *I wonder if you dreamt, if you loved.*

When I reminisce with my sisters, I wonder about your memories. *Were any of them joyful?*

While I watch the kids playing, imagining who they'll be when they're older, I wonder,
Did you miss your family? Did you ever meet them? Did any of them live a full life or was it cut short like yours?

In the moments where the sun is shining, *I wonder about your life in the dark.*

I wonder about *all that's done in the dark and all who are kept in the dark* so that you'll never see the sun.

I wonder, *what would your sun feel like?*

And I wonder,
When one is deprived of something that belongs to us all,
would they recognize it?

On a slaughter truck or in a crate,
the sun is either a death sentence or the only kindness you've ever known.

Mmm, here comes the sun. I wonder...

Do you?

BE THE SUN

I used to be scared of ghosts but my mom always said to fear
people instead / She said that / ghosts are just lost souls
trying to find their place, but / humans harm.
I never felt this truth until I learned what monsters we are

The contraptions we've made to enslave each other
Structures designed to keep us divided
A hopeless system meant to distract us
Bereft of our humanity,
We are the villains in bedtime stories
We are the captors of the innocent

We create the idea of freedom only to ensure we never have
it / Imprisoned, beaten and raped
Give me one good reason why
You're a slave meant to recognize your master
Bow down so you can't figure out how to escape
How did we let this get so far?
How did we allow and perpetuate the concept of other?

Humans or non-humans,
We focus on our differences like color, status and species,
Though we are the same in all the ways that matter

Don't we crave friendship? / Don't we understand what a
broken heart feels like? / Don't we recognize the sound of
someone crying out for a loved one?

We can't exist without water / we cannot live without love
It is the very air we breathe, the sun that sustains all life
We can never be free if we are oppressors / For to be one or
the other would still leave us anchored to an / unforgiving
world

Who created the rules and why do we still follow them?
Break those chains, smash the isms / There is no other.

It is simply that I am you and you are me

They say the eyes betray us / When you look into their eyes, do you see a mirror / a reflection of one being?
Or do you look away in shame for all that you are and all that you have tolerated?

Until you speak up and make a change / You are not only complicit / you remain the monster you teach your children to fear / The scariest part that isn't a tale is that they, too, become their / greatest fears

Rather than acting like other animals, whose love knows no bounds / We behave, instead, as humans do:
Reckless, destructive, and unforgiving
What legacy should we leave behind for the next generation / if we don't plunder first for disgracing our
Mother Earth and all of her creatures?

We'll have the future to answer to.

When asked what you've done to end the suffering,
When asked who you chose to be,
When asked if your decisions hurt or helped,
What would you say for yourself?

Were you a protector or destroyer?

In your care, because of your choices did someone love or languish? / As a human, cause no harm. / Don't be the ghosts of regret that will haunt those we leave behind.

Instead,

BE THE SUN.

Acknowledgements

Thank you, mom, dad, and my sisters. I would like to think that I have inherited all of your best parts. I recognize the human in all of you, and I hope this book will help you see me.

Mom, I spoke to you about this book before it was published. I was afraid of how you'd react, but you surprised me in the best way. I'm so glad our love transcends generational trauma and misunderstandings, enough that we can talk about and learn from them. Thank you for the translations!

Fofinho, thank you for helping me get this far – we have been growing since we met, and we have lifetimes more to go. You are my home and adventure. I love you.

Muschis & Furf, you are my light and blessing in this unbearable world. You know what makes and breaks me and, for that, I am both sorry and grateful. I will never be alone and I will never feel lonely as long as I have you all in my life.

Iraina, my bf, made me feel so safe that I shared my love letters with you long before I shared my work with anyone else. True to your nature, you always encouraged me to keep writing. Thank you for always loving and supporting me!

Justin, you only got 1 shot, do not miss your chance, don't blow this opportunity comes 1x in a lifetime, you #bidet.

Queens Poetic Alchemy Collective (QPAC) / Faizan / Steve - You are the first safe space where I dared to share myself. I challenged myself to do what terrifies me, and I found you at the perfect moment. You saved me. Rox, thank you for pushing for and then witnessing that first moment.

Speak the Word, VOICE 4 Change, The Well World, The Word is Write (WIW), - You are not just groups or organizations. You are all made up of powerful individuals that have fostered a space where safety is a certainty. You nurture strength, honesty, and artistry. Some of my favorite pieces were borne in your spaces, and my workshops are heavily inspired by all of you.

Cafe Writers - Another safe space where talent is abundant. I almost talked myself out of performing, fearing my own inadequacy. Still, I shared one of my favorite pieces, "These Hands," and you (unknowingly) validated my leap of faith by choosing (and keeping) it as your Poem of the Month for about three months.

Shane Manier, the founder of both The National Poetry Month Summit and Guerilla Poets, thank you for my stunning cover. I love every detail and every story it tells. You brought my vision to life and had the patience and compassion to incorporate all my ideas down to the minutiae.

Marissa Prada, founder of Read or Green Books (RGB) and WIW. The first time we met (and actually remembered our interaction), you mentioned that you were a publisher. This was both exciting and nerve-wracking to hear since I had just been rejected by multiple outlets. I performed and, almost immediately after, you asked if I was published; and I said something like, *"No, but if someone wants to publish me, let me know!"* I emailed you that night, and the rest is history.

Thank you for seeing me, resonating with my art, and guiding, teaching and believing in me enough to invite me into the Fierce Fifteam! Your belief in me, which lead to this book, helped advance my journey of believing in myself. Working on my manuscript was so challenging, and I appreciate every lesson (for the next book, am I right?)!

Last, but not least, I would like to thank myself. That's right. This is different and uncomfortable, but I deserve it! I was/am in disbelief even up until this moment, but I worked hard for it.

I feel the fear and do it anyway. I hope you all do, too.

About the Author

The first time Maureen performed at an open mic, she was fulfilling a promise to herself to "do something that terrified [her]." Though she had written here and there since she was in her early teens, Maureen's first time performing was with the Queens Poetic Alchemy Collective (QPAC) in 2017.

She continued to write poetry, but her focus shifted to other forms of activism for the next few years. Devoting herself to learning about and dismantling systemic oppression of all beings, Maureen found inspiration in both hope and devastation.

When the pandemic hit, Maureen reconnected with QPAC and attended their virtual open mics regularly. This became a release as she decidedly began her journey of healing and self-discovery.

Maureen hosts workshops with The Word is Write, on the 2nd and 4th Tuesday of the month; and some open mics and workshops with Speak the Word on Saturdays.

Maureen's work has been featured on Waxy and Poetic, Harness Magazine, Independent Media Institute, and The Well World, and she has her own blog. One of her favorite pieces, "These Hands," was published in Grassroots Theatre Company's Winter Zine and featured as Cafe Writers' Poem of the Month from February to April 2022.

Maureen is the founder of Leave in Peace, an initiative focused on assisting and highlighting the reality of slaughterhouse workers. She has organized food and clothing drives since before the pandemic and has helped distribute over 1,500 meals and over 1,000 pounds of clothing, shoes, and toiletries. To support her work, visit: linktr.ee/LeaveInPeace.

Maureen is a campaign organizer for Slaughter Free NYC, which aims to shut down slaughterhouses in NYC for the benefit of communities that are directly exposed to them, as well as the non-human animals that are destroyed in them.

Maureen advocates for both human and non-human animals and asserts that all oppression is connected. In alignment with the idea that none of us are free unless all of us are free, Maureen hopes to inspire the pursuit of collective liberation through her writing.

Maureen P. Medina